Materials Needed

Materials for each session vary from Bible story to Bible story. The following lists detail the items needed for every session as well as the items needed uniquely for each session.

For Every Session

- ☆ *Activity Center Signs,* "Good News Galaxy" and "Praise Phrase"
- ☆ *Bible Storyteller & Sound Effects CD*
- ☆ CD player
- ☆ Bible
- ☆ *Bible Storyteller*
- ☆ *Solar Key Chain* (one per child)

 Session 1

- ☆ *Decorating Transparencies,* "God's Creatures I & II," and "Space Items I"
- ☆ spotlight or floodlight
- ☆ string and hooks, or black sheet
- ☆ large cardboard box labeled "IN THE BEGINNING"
- ☆ material in shades of blue (light blue for the sky, darker blue for the water), brown (the ground), and green (grass)
- ☆ artificial plants and flowers (if possible, use those listed in poem)
- ☆ posterboard
- ☆ marker
- ☆ Session One Bible verse printed on posterboard or the poster from the *Decorating Poster Pak*
- ☆ Session One *Scripture Treasures:* Earth 3-D card (one per child)
- ☆ stuffed or plastic birds, fish, and animals (if possible, use those listed in poem)
- ☆ camera (optional)
- ☆ butcher paper
- ☆ paint
- ☆ scissors

 Session 2

- ☆ *Decorating Transparency,* "Cave at Mt. Horeb"
- ☆ plants and rocks
- ☆ large brown or gray sheet
- ☆ scissors
- ☆ three letter-size pieces of card stock
- ☆ marker
- ☆ two box or stand fans
- ☆ six sheets of posterboard, folded with accordion folds into six large fans
- ☆ four-foot lengths of red and yellow crepe paper streamers (two or three per child)
- ☆ Session Two Bible verse printed on posterboard or the poster from the *Decorating Poster Pak*
- ☆ Session Two *Scripture Treasures:* Moon 3-D card (one per child)
- ☆ twelve white paper plates (one set per group of three or four children)

 Session 3

- ☆ *Decorating Transparencies,* "Biblical Town" and "Signpost" ("Sychar")
- ☆ plants and rocks
- ☆ thirty-two brown paper grocery bags
- ☆ newspapers (for stuffing bags)
- ☆ clear packing tape
- ☆ four small plastic buckets
- ☆ rope
- ☆ water
- ☆ paper cups (one per child)
- ☆ white carnation or daisy in plain water
- ☆ white carnation or daisy in blue water
- ☆ Session Three Bible verse printed on posterboard or the poster from the *Decorating Poster Pak*
- ☆ Session Three *Scripture Treasures:* Stars 3-D card (one per child)
- ☆ ten stars cut from yellow posterboard
- ☆ marker

...black fabric
- ☆ ten safety pins
- ☆ ten pieces of string, varying from three to four feet in length
- ☆ ten paper clips

 Session 4

- ☆ *Decorating Transparencies,* "Biblical Town" and "Signpost" ("Jericho")
- ☆ plants and rocks
- ☆ blindfolds (one per child)
- ☆ Session Four Bible verse printed on posterboard or the poster from the *Decorating Poster Pak*
- ☆ Session Four *Scripture Treasures:* Comet 3-D card (one per child)
- ☆ seven cardboard circles, two feet in diameter
- ☆ aluminum foil
- ☆ permanent marker

 Session 5

- ☆ *Decorating Transparencies,* "Biblical House" and "Signpost" ("Emmaus")
- ☆ plants and rocks
- ☆ table and chairs
- ☆ bread (enough for everyone to have a small piece)
- ☆ Session Five Bible verse printed on posterboard or the poster from the *Decorating Poster Pak*
- ☆ Session Five *Scripture Treasures:* Supernova 3-D card (one per child)
- ☆ large, dark-colored sheet or shower curtain
- ☆ silver or yellow paint
- ☆ permanent marker
- ☆ small stars cut from yellow or silver paper
- ☆ washable markers

Bible Drama Option
Using One to Four Adults Per Drama

With this leader book you can choose to tell the story with a single storyteller (see description on page 7) or in a dramatic adaptation. Plan ahead by reading each lesson and determining, based on the resources at your church, which method will work best for you. Either or both forms of presentation can be used throughout your VBS.

Some of the stories told at the Good News Galaxy may be familiar to your cadets. By using these storytelling models you will be able give the children an opportunity to experience the stories in a brand new way.

Preparation for each session of the Good News Galaxy is key to its success. The people you recruit to play parts in the dramas need to familiarize themselves with the stories in advance so they can play their parts without scripts in their hands. The lines do not need to be memorized exactly as written; it is more important to interact with the children to draw them into the action. Use the scripts as a guide to follow while telling the story.

Try to involve as many children as possible in each story. If you cannot use everyone, be sure to choose different children for each session.

Decorating can be as simple or as elaborate as time and funds allow. A list of props and staging ideas can be found at the beginning of each session. Keep in mind that children have a wonderful sense of imagination, and they can see a great deal into the simplest of staging. One test church used an empty room with a single storyteller; his voice and interaction with the children brought each Bible story to life. Another test church used extensive props and drama characters. In each scenario the children were drawn into the story and engaged in the Bible message.

Props are a wonderful way to bring the story to life, regardless of how complex your scenery is. Use the background sound effects from the *Bible Storyteller & Sound Effects CD* once you enter the Bible room to create a suitable atmosphere for the stories.

The full lesson plan for each session's Bible storytelling time is in this book. If you want to make copies of the script portion of each drama, downloadable PDF files are located on the *Bible Storyteller & Sound Effects CD*. Place the CD in your computer and download the printed drama scripts for each session.

Bible Story Characters

Session One: Storyteller

Session Two: Elijah

Session Three: Jesus
Samaritan Woman
Jesus' Disciples

Session Four: Jesus
Blind Beggar

Session Five: Jesus
Cleopas
Other Disciple

Decorating can be as simple or elaborate as time and funds allow.

Single Storyteller Option
Using One Adult Storyteller

Using the single Bible storyteller option is a great way for the children to feel like they have really gotten to know a Bible character. The characters will talk to the children about how their experiences with God have made an impression in their lives. Even with a familiar story, this approach can give children a different perspective that they have never heard before.

The single storyteller narrations are available at the end of each session. Scripts are also available on the *Bible Storyteller & Sound Effects CD*, found in the *Starter Kit* or available for purchase separately. Place the CD in your computer and download the storyteller versions for each session. Place the CD in your CD player to hear the stories being told.

With this option, a separate leader can greet the children as they enter the room. This person reviews the stories they have already heard and prepares the children for what they are going experience on this mission. Then this leader introduces them to the Bible character who will tell them the Bible story.

Preparation for each session of the Good News Galaxy is key to its success. The people you recruit to be the storytellers need to familiarize themselves with the stories so they can play their parts without scripts in their hands. The lines do not need to be memorized exactly as written; it is more important to interact with the children to draw them into the action. Use the scripts as a guide to follow while telling the story. Each storyteller should listen to the *Bible Storyteller & Sound Effects CD* to hear how the characters can be portrayed.

Preparation is the key to success.

Storyteller Presentation Tips

★ Practice telling the story.
★ Be dynamic and become the character.
★ Learn the story incident by incident and not word for word.
★ Use your whole body when telling the story.

Session Overviews

Session One: The children build a creation scene as they hear the creation story told in the form of a poem.

Session Two: The children meet Elijah, who tells them of his encounter with God at Mt. Horeb.

Session Three: The children meet a Samaritan woman who describes her encounter with Jesus at Jacob's well.

Session Four: The children meet a blind beggar who talks about his encounter with Jesus on the road to Jericho. Jesus gave the blind beggar his sight.

Session Five: The children will meet Cleopas, who recounts his encounter with Jesus as he was walking with a friend on the road to Emmaus.

Photo: Meaghan Porter

Mission: Creation of the Universe (Genesis 1:1–2:4)

★ Materials

Mission
Creation of the Universe
(Genesis 1:1–2:4)

Bible Booster
The earth is the LORD's and all that is in it, the world, and those who live in it.
(Psalm 24:1, NRSV)

Praise Phrase
Our God is wonderful! Praise God!

Color of the Day
Green

For every session
☆ *Activity Center Signs,* "Good News Galaxy" and "Praise Phrase"
☆ *Bible Storyteller & Sound Effects CD*

☆ CD player
☆ Bible
☆ *Bible Storyteller*
☆ *Solar Key Chain* (one per child)

For this session
☆ *Decorating Transparencies,* "God's Creatures I," "God's Creatures II," and "Space Items I"
☆ spotlight or floodlight
☆ string and hooks, or black sheet
☆ large cardboard box labeled "IN THE BEGINNING"
☆ material in shades of blue (light blue for the sky, darker blue for the water), brown (the ground), and green (grass)

☆ artificial plants and flowers (if possible, use those listed in poem)
☆ posterboard
☆ marker
☆ Session One Bible verse printed on posterboard or the poster from the *Decorating Poster Pak*
☆ Session One *Scripture Treasures:* Earth 3-D card (one per child)

☆ stuffed or plastic birds, fish, and animals (if possible, use those listed in poem)
☆ camera (optional)
☆ butcher paper
☆ paint
☆ scissors

Photo: Lima Jo Simon

Creating the Atmosphere

Bible Adventure Room

★ Post the "Good News Galaxy" sign outside the room. Post the "Praise Phrase" sign with today's Praise Phrase ("Our God is wonderful! Praise God!") in a prominent place inside the room.

★ Tell this story in a room that has no natural light, such as one on an indoor corridor or in a basement. If the room does have windows, cover them with dark blankets, black plastic sheeting, or black paper to block out as much of the light as possible. Clear the room of any decorations, posters, or furniture. Make it as empty as possible. Optional: Photograph the empty room.

★ Place the floodlight in a corner of the room.

★ Hang string from the ceiling and place hooks or paper clips at the ends so children can hang the sky material, clouds, sun, moon, stars, and birds as they listen to the poem. Alternatively, hang a sheet along one wall and pin or tape the items to it as the story is told.

★ Use the "Space Items I" *Decorating Transparency* to create the clouds, stars, moon, and sun on posterboard or styrofoam. You could also use a white ball for the moon and a yellow ball for the sun; just be sure that the children can hang the end product from the hooks.

★ Use the "God's Creatures I" and "God's Creatures II" *Decorating Transparencies* to create birds, fish, and animals on posterboard.

★ Put the cardboard box in the center of the room. Layer the remaining Bible story items inside it so that the material is on the top and the animals are on the bottom.

Drama Characters and Costumes

No costumes are needed for this session.

Bible Booster Challenge

★ Use the "Space Items I" *Decorating Transparency* to create a large Earth, centered on the butcher paper. Be sure to leave plenty of space around Earth. Paint Earth.

★ Starting at the North Pole, write the Bible verse and the verse reference in a circle surrounding Earth.

★ Cut Earth and the words into eight wedges (like pizza slices). Don't worry if words or letters are broken apart.

★ In preparation for Session Three, place a white carnation or daisy in a vase of water dyed blue with food coloring. Set aside. Keeping the flower in the food coloring for forty-eight hours made for a successful demonstration in Session Three.

★ If you create Earth on blue butcher paper instead of white, you need to paint only the land green, as the water will already be blue. A small timesaver, perhaps, but in VBS preparation, every minute counts!

Please note that there is no separate single storyteller version for this session. If you are using the single storyteller method and want to read the story to the children without their involvement, simply read the poem aloud. Use the *Bible Storyteller & Sound Effects CD* to assist with the poem. Alternatively, you may play the narrative from the CD (track #1).

⭐Story Starter

STORYTELLER: *(Meet the children outside the Bible storytelling room.)* **Welcome, cadets, to the Good News Galaxy! I'm Mission Specialist** *(name)*, **and I'll be guiding you through each of your cosmic Bible adventures. Each day we're going to have a close encounter with our wonderful, incredible, amazing, magnificent, and awesome God. Are you excited?** *(Yes!)* **Are you ready?** *(Yes!)* **Then here we go!**

(With great excitement, lead the children into the room, but express disappointment when you see that the room is empty.) **Well, this isn't very exciting, or wonderful, or incredible—or much of anything. There are no pictures or decorations or fun things to do. Do you think we're in the right place?** *(Let the children answer.)*

(If the kids have not pointed out the box, draw their attention to it.) **"IN THE BEGINNING."** **Those words sound familiar. Where have I heard them before?** *(Older children may recognize the words from Genesis. If they do, you can answer with a noncommittal "maybe." Otherwise, continue.)* **Well, since there's nothing else to do in here, I guess we should open the box. What do you think?**

(Open the box and look inside.) **Oh, now I understand! Wow, this is wonderful! OK, I'm going to need everyone's help. I need each of you to take something from the box until it's empty.** *(Depending on the size of your group, some children may need to take more than one item.)* **When you have your items, find a seat around the edge of the room.**

Did you know that many, many, many, *many* years ago, God looked out at the whole universe, and it was as empty as this room? The universe isn't empty now, is it? *(Let the children respond.)* **We're going to find out how God made *everything*!**

Here's our mission, cadets: We're going to create the whole world— right in this room! I will tell you when you need to add your item to the scene. But as we create, I need you to be very quiet so that you can hear what happened.

(Turn off the lights.) **As soon as everyone is quiet and still, we'll begin.**

(Read aloud the poem on the following pages. Direct the children to add their items to the scene as indicated. See the Teacher Tip for information about the single storyteller version.)

In the beginning

 Today's Cosmic Adventure

Storyteller: **It starts like this: older than old,
darker than dark, colder than cold.
A single sound swept round and round:
the rhythmic breath of God.**

Ask the children to make the sound of God's breath.

**This Spirit-breath was full of might,
and when God breathed the first word: "Light!"—
at God's command, as God had planned,
light blazed and burst and glowed.**

Turn on the spotlight. Play CD track #2, "Light & Sky."

**Beholding light, God named it "day,"
and "night" was what it pushed away.
God watched light spread, then smiled and said,
"What I have made is good."**

**The first day passed. God spoke anew.
"A sky!" God said. "A dome of blue
will draw the line in my design
between the waters deep."**

Children drape the light blue material from the ceiling.

**God twirled a finger, spun a cloud,
then two, then more. God said aloud,
"This world of mine is really fine!"
The second day was done.**

The children hang up the clouds.

**The third day dawned, and God proclaimed
the lower waters should be named.
God called them "seas," and then with ease
God moved the waves aside.**

Play CD track #3, "Waves."
Children place the dark blue material on the floor.

**With twinkling eyes and potter's hands,
God shaped the soil and sprinkled sands
as fine as hair in places where
the waters once had stood.**

The children place the brown material on the floor in the middle of the dark blue material.

**"I think I'll call the new land 'earth,'"
God said, then told it to give birth
to plants with seeds and fruits and trees
and flowers, leaves, and ferns.**

The children place the plants and flowers in the scene.

**Asparagus, an apple green,
a rose, a grape, a lima bean,
a branch of pine, an ivy vine—
God touched each one in turn.**

The fourth day God peered into space.   *Play CD track #4, "Space."*
"Oh, wow!" God said. "It's just the place
to scatter far and wide the stars
in galaxies galore!"

A comet there, an asteroid here,
a planet shaped into a sphere,
the moon, the sun—it's so much fun
to make a universe!   *Children hang sun, moon, and stars.*

The fifth day God made ducks and hens   *Play CD track #5, "Birds & Fish."*
and larks and loons and pelicans,
and other birds with names absurd,
like whippoorwill and finch.   *Children add birds to the scene.*

And then the oceans came alive
with eel that wriggle, whales that dive,
and octopi and squid so shy
they're hardly ever seen.   *Children add sea creatures to the scene.*

"Now listen, birds, and listen, fish!"
God said, "I have a special wish:
that you will go and overflow
the world that I have made."

The sixth day opened full of sounds   *Play CD track #6, "Animal Sounds."*
from pigs and cows and basset hounds,
from rats and bats and kitty cats.
God's animals are loud!   *Children add animals to the scene.*

But still God added to the list,
with bees that buzzed and snakes that hissed,
with butterflies of every size,
and bouncing kangaroos.   *Children add more animals to the scene.*

God could have stopped to take a break,
but God had something more to make:
"I need some friends whom I can send
to do my work on earth."

A gentle breath then left God's lips.   *Ask the children to make the sound of God's breath.*
It carved out feet and legs and hips
and chest and face: the human race
was what God brought to life.   *Children take their places in the scene.*

God told the humans, "Yes, it's true
I made this whole world just for you.
To you I give all things that live,
all creatures great and small.

"I made you in my image, see?
You can create and you are free.
Now go explore from shore to shore
this gift I made for you."

At last creation's work was done.
The seventh day had just begun.
God loved the world, and that love swirled
throughout the planet Earth.

"It's time to stop for now," God said.
"Although much more work lies ahead,
this day I've blessed as one of rest,
a Sabbath for us all."

So all we know and all we see—
the largest, farthest galaxy,
the smallest flea, and you and me—
it all belongs to God.

Let everything that has breath praise
our God for those six busy days
so God can hear our joyful cheer:
Praise God! Praise God! Praise God!

Photo: Staff

Encourage the children to say "Praise God!" with you. (Optional: Take a few pictures of the children and their creation before asking them to have a seat.)

(Share this tidbit with your class.)

Apollo 8 was the first manned mission to the moon. On Christmas Eve, 1968, Apollo 8's astronauts took turns reading from Genesis 1 during a live broadcast from space back to Earth.

Teacher Tip

You can find audio clips from this Christmas Eve broadcast on the Internet. Play the clips as time allows.

Bible Wrap-Up

Teacher Tip

An alternative title for the Old Testament is the Hebrew Scriptures. Use the name that is most acceptable in your church.

STORYTELLER: **Do you remember today's Praise Phrase? I think now is a great time to use it. Our God is wonderful!** *(Praise God!)*

The story you were just a part of comes from the Bible. The Bible is divided into two sections, the Old Testament and the New Testament. The creation story is the first story in Genesis, the first book of the Old Testament. In other words, the creation story is the first story in the whole Bible. *(Show the children where the story is in the Bible.)*

The word Genesis means "beginning," and the very first words of the story are "In the beginning." Do you remember where we saw those words? *(The words are on the box.)* **Right! The creation story tells about what happened "in the beginning."**

The Bible says that God worked on creation for six days. Let's see if we can remember what God did on each day. *(Walk the children through each day. Ask them to remember what changed in their creation scene for each day; if necessary, you can read parts of the poem again. On posterboard, write down each day's work as you discuss it. Your list could look like this:*

Day 1: Light
Day 2: Sky and clouds
Day 3: Oceans, land, plants, flowers
Day 4: Sun, moon, stars, planets
Day 5: Birds and fish
Day 6: Animals and humans)

What did God do on the seventh day? *(God rested.)* **That's right. Wouldn't you want to rest after you made all of creation?** *(Yes!)* **God called this day of rest a sabbath, which means "rest."**

Life Application

STORYTELLER: **Let's talk about gift-giving. What does it mean when someone gives you a gift?** *(It means that person cares about you or loves you.)* **How do you feel when someone gives you a gift?** *(Happy, excited, thankful)* **How do you treat a gift?** *(We take special care of it.)*

What does it mean that God gave the world to humans as a gift? *(It means that God loves humans very much.)* **How should we treat that gift?** *(We have to take care of it.)* **What can we do to take care of that gift?** *(We can recycle, try to use less water and less electricity, plant trees or other living things, and care for and protect the animals.)* **We call**

taking care of the earth this way **"being green."**

How does it make you feel that God has given us such an amazing gift? *(Happy, excited, thankful, amazed)* **When you feel happy about something that God has done, you can show it in many different ways. You can tell God thank you, either aloud or in a silent prayer. You can sing for God or dance for God. You can even tell other people about the wonderful thing God has done. We call all of these things praising God.**

Let's show God how happy we are that God made creation just for us. Our God is wonderful! *(Praise God!)*

Bible Booster Challenge

Materials
☆ *Decorating Transparency,* "Space Items I"
☆ butcher paper
☆ paint
☆ markers
☆ scissors

STORYTELLER: **Each day we're going to learn a Bible Booster, a Bible verse that will help us remember something about God that is worthy of praise. These verses come from the Book of Psalms, which is a part of the Old Testament of the Bible that contains poems and songs people use to praise God. We'll also complete a Bible Booster Challenge to help us learn the Bible verse.**

Today's Bible Booster is Psalm 24:1: "The earth is the LORD's and all that is in it, the world, and those who live in it." As we've seen today, God made everything, and everything belongs to God.

Here I have eight giant puzzle pieces. When you put them in the right order, you'll discover today's verse and something related to it.

(Let the children work together to assemble the puzzle pieces so that the verse and Earth are revealed.)

You made planet Earth! Imagine all the different places on Earth: hot deserts, freezing cold Arctic ice, rainforests, mountains, grassy fields, oceans that are miles deep. God made all of that! Now imagine all the animals in those places: camels in the deserts, polar bears at the North Pole, parrots in the rainforest, eagles in the mountains, cows in the field, sharks in the ocean. God made all of those, too. And God made every single person—all six billion of us, including you!

Let our wonderful planet be a reminder to you of our wonderful God.

(Give each child today's Scripture Treasure. *Review the information on the back of the card, and point out how the picture on the front is a reminder that God created Earth.)*

Preparation

★ Use the *Decorating Transparency* to create a large Earth, centered on the butcher paper. Be sure to leave plenty of space around Earth. Paint Earth.

★ Starting at the North Pole, write the Bible Booster and the verse reference in a circle surrounding Earth.

★ Cut Earth and the words into eight wedges (like pizza slices). Don't worry if words or letters are broken apart.

Bible Booster

The earth is the LORD's and all that is in it, the world, and those who live in it. (Psalm 24:1, NRSV)

Test Church Tip

This session ran long, so consider moving the Bible Booster Challenge to reflection time.

Teacher Tip

If your group is large, you may want to make several Earths and have the children solve the puzzle in smaller groups.

Photo: Lima Jo Simon

Sign the Scripture

Let's learn the Bible Booster using sign language.

(Teach the sign language and use it as you practice the Bible verse with the children. If time is running short, plan to teach the sign language during reflection time. Reproduce the page and give it to each reflection time pilot. Video of a leader saying the verse using sign language can be found on the Adventure Video DVD/CD-ROM.)

EARTH

Make a fist with your left hand. Place your right thumb and middle finger on the back of the left hand, near the wrist. Rock the right hand from side to side.

LORD

Make an L with your right hand and bring it from left shoulder to right hip.

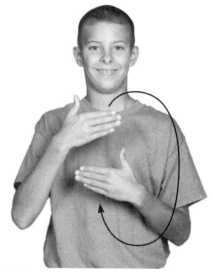

ALL

With your left palm facing the body, circle your open right hand out and around the left hand. Finish with the back of the right hand pressed against the left palm.

WORLD

With three fingers of each hand extended, circle the right hand forward and down, ending with the right hand next to the left, thumbs touching.

LIVE

Use index fingers of both hands to make L shapes, with index fingers pointing toward each other, at your waist. Draw your hands in this position up your chest.

Photos: Matt Huesmann

Galactic Blast: A Cosmic Adventure Praising God!

Closing Prayer

STORYTELLER: **It's time to leave the Good News Galaxy. Before you go, I have a mission for you based on today's story. We talked about Earth as God's gift God gave to us, and we thought of ways to "be green" and take care of that gift. Your mission to accomplish when you go home is to do something small to take care of God's creation. How do you think you can do that?** *(Let the children share ideas.)* **When you visit the Good News Galaxy tomorrow, you can tell me what you did.**

Let's close with a prayer. After I pray a sentence, I would like you to respond with, "We praise you, God!"

Let's pray.

LEADER: **Dear God, we're so excited to spend time together learning about you at GALACTIC BLAST.**

ALL: **We praise you, God!**

LEADER: **We're so amazed that you made the sun and the moon and the stars for us.**

ALL: **We praise you, God!**

LEADER: **We're so thankful that you made the sky and the water and the land for us.**

ALL: **We praise you, God!**

LEADER: **We're so happy that you made all the animals for us.**

ALL: **We praise you, God!**

LEADER: **Most of all, we're so blessed that you made us!**

ALL: **We praise you, God!**

LEADER: **Help us take care of the earth and each other, and guide us as we continue on our cosmic adventure.**

ALL: **We praise you, God!**

LEADER: **We pray all of this to you, our wonderful God. Amen.**

(Have the children help you put the items for the Bible story back in the box in preparation for the next group.)

We praise you, God!

Session 2

Mission
Elijah at Mt. Horeb
(1 Kings 19:4-18)

Bible Booster
But for me it is good to be near God.
(Psalm 73:28a, NRSV)

Praise Phrase
Our God is incredible! Praise God!

Color of the Day
Red

Mission: Elijah at Mt. Horeb (1 Kings 19:4-18)

★ Materials

For every session
- ☆ *Activity Center Signs,* "Good News Galaxy" and "Praise Phrase"
- ☆ *Bible Storyteller & Sound Effects CD*
- ☆ CD player
- ☆ Bible
- ☆ *Bible Storyteller*
- ☆ Bible story costumes
- ☆ *Solar Key Chain* (one per child)

For this session
- ☆ *Decorating Transparency,* "Cave at Mt. Horeb"
- ☆ plants and rocks
- ☆ large brown or gray sheet
- ☆ scissors
- ☆ three letter-size pieces of card stock
- ☆ marker
- ☆ two box or stand fans
- ☆ six sheets of posterboard, folded with accordion folds into six large fans
- ☆ four-foot lengths of red and yellow crepe paper streamers (two or three per child)
- ☆ Session Two Bible verse printed on posterboard or the poster from the *Decorating Poster Pak*
- ☆ Session Two *Scripture Treasures:* Moon 3-D card (one per child)
- ☆ twelve white paper plates (one set per group of three or four children)

Photo: Lima Jo Simon

Creating the Atmosphere

Bible Adventure Room

★ Post the "Good News Galaxy" sign outside the room. Post the "Praise Phrase" sign with today's Praise Phrase ("Our God is incredible! Praise God!") in a prominent place inside the room.

★ On one of the walls, trace, paint, and hang the scene from the "Cave at Mt. Horeb" *Decorating Transparency*. If possible, cover the entire wall with the full landscape so the children feel they are in front of the cave when they step into the classroom. See page 8 of the *Decorating Guide* for detailed instructions for creating backdrops from transparencies.

★ Build the cave forward into the room by hanging a brown or gray sheet from the ceiling, parallel to the backdrop and a few feet in front of it. Cut an arch-like opening in the sheet to match the cave opening on the transparency. Add plants and rocks around the front of the cave opening to give the impression of the wilderness in front of the cave.

★ Label one piece of card stock with a "W," one with an "E," and one with an "F."

Drama Characters and Costumes

★ Elijah: Over a long tunic in a muted color, wear a robe tied with a sash.

Bible Booster Challenge

★ Identify one of the paper plates as "Earth," either by coloring it like a globe or by labeling it.

★ Write one word from the Bible Booster on each of ten remaining plates. Write the Bible verse reference on the last plate. These eleven plates represent the moon as it orbits Earth.

⭐ Story Starter

(Welcome the children in front of the cave opening.)

STORYTELLER: **Welcome back to the Good News Galaxy, where we're learning great things about God. This week's cosmic adventures show us many reasons to praise our wonderful God!**

In our first session, what did we see God do? *(God created the universe.)* **God started with nothing and created everything in the universe, from the farthest galaxy to the tiniest grain of sand. God is wonderful!** *(Praise God!)*

You had a special mission to complete when you went home. Who wants to share how you took care of God's creation? *(Allow a few moments for sharing.)*

The creation story shows that our God is powerful, a God of amazing works. But God is not a far-away God who lives somewhere in space. God is very close and very personal. The same God who created all the stars and planets created you, too, and God is with you wherever you go.

In today's Bible adventure, I need all of you to help act out three natural events found in creation. First, you will be a strong wind. We'll use the help of a few fans, but I also want six of you to use these large posterboard fans. *(Pass out the fans.)* **Those of you who do not have a fan can make the sound of the wind. When I raise this "W" sign, make the wind blow. When I lower the sign, stop.** *(Practice a few times.)*

That was a great wind! Now you're going to be an earthquake. Has anyone here ever experienced an earthquake? *(Let the children answer.)* **I want some of you to make a rumbling sound.** *(Assign this role to a few children.)* **I need some of you to shake the rocks and the plants.** *(Assign this role to a few children.)* **Everyone else can stomp their feet as if rocks are falling. When I raise this "E" sign, I want you to make the earthquake. When I lower the sign, stop.** *(Practice a few times.)*

What a super earthquake! The last event for you to act out is a roaring fire. We need flames, right? *(Give each child two or three red or yellow streamers.)* **To create the fire, let's huddle together and wave our streamers overhead. At the same time, make the sound of a roaring fire. When I raise this "F" sign, I want you to create a fire. When I lower the sign, stop.** *(Practice a few times.)*

We can find God in creation in everything we see. God is everywhere! But if God were going to talk to you, what do you think God would sound like? How do you think God would appear? *(Let the children answer.)* **In today's adventure, we will learn how our great God and Creator talked to the prophets in the Old Testament.**

Remember how the Bible has two parts, the Old Testament and the New Testament? In the Old Testament, God had a chosen group of people named the Israelites. During the time that today's story takes place, King Ahab and Queen Jezebel ruled

Teacher Tip

If you are working with a large group, divide it into three smaller groups and assign each one of the natural events.

over the Israelites. Queen Jezebel was not an Israelite herself; she was from another country. The king and queen allowed the Israelite people to worship idols, or fake gods, instead of the one true God. This did not please God.

God had a prophet among the people whose job it was to tell people what God wanted them to know. This prophet's name was Elijah. With God's help, Elijah fought the prophets of Baal, one of the idols. Elijah worked to bring the Israelites back to believing in just the one true God, which made Queen Jezebel very angry. She sent a message to Elijah that she was going to kill him.

Now Elijah is on the run. He is afraid. He has even asked God if he might die. God has a message for Elijah, and you're going to help bring that message to him. So when Elijah arrives, pay attention so you will know when to add the wind, the earthquake, and the fire. Are you ready? *(Be sure everyone is prepared.)*

Let's be quiet now. I think Elijah is coming this way.

(If you are using the single storyteller version on page 27, begin it here and pick up the lesson at the Bible Wrap-Up on page 23.)

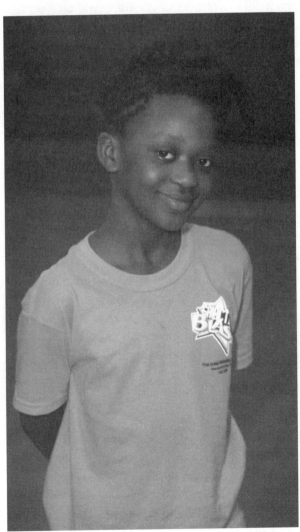

Photo: Matt Huesmann

Today's Cosmic Adventure

(Elijah arrives, tired and out of breath. He does not notice the children. He sits at the opening of the cave.)

ELIJAH: **Oh, I am so tired! I have been traveling for so long! Maybe I can rest in this cave. I know Queen Jezebel wants to kill me. I have nowhere to go and no one to protect me. I feel so lost. Oh God, I am praying to you, please just let me die.**

(Wait a moment in silence, then play track #8 to hear the voice of God.)

GOD: **Elijah, what are you doing here?**

ELIJAH: *(Looking around the room)* **Lord, I am your servant. I have served only you. But your people, the Israelites, have broken their promises to you. They have killed your prophets. I am the only one left who truly believes in you, and the queen is trying to kill me!**

(Play track #9 for God's lines.)

GOD: **Elijah, step out on the mountain. I am about to pass by.**

(Elijah, shocked, stands up, steps to the middle of the room, and looks around. The Storyteller raises the "W" sign to signal the children to begin the wind. Turn on the fans. Play track #10 to hear the wind.)

ELIJAH: **God, are you here? Are you in the wind?**

(The Storyteller lowers the "W" sign to stop the wind. Turn off the fans and stop the CD. Allow a moment of silence. The Storyteller then raises the "E" sign to signal the children to begin the earthquake. Play track #11 to hear the earthquake.)

ELIJAH: *(Frightened)* **God, are you here?**

(The Storyteller lowers the "E" sign to stop the earthquake. Allow a moment of silence. The Storyteller raises the "F" sign to signal the children to begin the fire. Play track #12 to hear the fire.)

ELIJAH: *(Looking at the fire)* **God, are you in the fire?**

(The Storyteller lowers the "F" sign to stop the fire. Allow the room to go completely silent as Elijah looks around. Play track #13 for God's line.)

GOD: *(Softly)* **Elijah, why are you here?**

ELIJAH: **Lord, I have served only you. But your people, the Israelites, have broken their promises to you. They have killed your prophets. I am the only one left, and people are trying to kill me!**

(Play track #14 for God's lines.)

GOD: *(Still whispering)* **Elijah, I need you to go back to work. Return to an area near Damascus, anoint a new king of Aram and a new king of Israel, and anoint a new prophet, Elisha. There are also seven thousand people alive who still believe in me.**

ELIJAH: **God, you have found me. I will do your work. I know you will take care of me and the rest of your people. There are seven thousand people who still believe in you! Our God is incredible!**

CHILDREN: **Praise God!**

(Elijah runs out of the room.)

Bible Wrap-Up

(Collect the props from the children.)

STORYTELLER: **Where do you think Elijah is going? Is he still running away from Queen Jezebel?** *(Elijah is going back to do God's work.)*

Elijah was a great prophet of God. You can read this story about him in the Old Testament, starting in 1 Kings 19:4. *(Show the children the Bible passage.)*

Elijah found himself with a big problem. The queen wanted to kill him! Even though he knew how great God is, Elijah ran away.

What did God do? *(God found Elijah and told him what to do.)*

God went to Elijah. God knew Elijah was afraid and running away.

Was God in the wind? *(No.)* **Was God in the earthquake?** *(No.)* **Was God in the fire?** *(No.)*

God showed God's power with the wind and the earthquake and the fire. But how did God communicate with Elijah? *(God whispered.)* **God used a quiet voice—some say "a still small voice"—to tell Elijah what to do.**

What instructions did God give Elijah? *(God told Elijah to name two kings and anoint a new prophet.)* **God sent Elijah back to work and back to the people. Elijah went, knowing that he was not alone.**

Life Application

STORYTELLER: **Have you ever felt afraid or alone?** *(Yes.)* **I think Elijah felt that way. He didn't think anyone could help him, but God reminded Elijah that he didn't have to face his problem alone.**

God never leaves our side. This is a great reason to praise God. Our God is incredible! *(Praise God!)*

What did we have to do to hear God? *(We needed to be quiet.)* **We needed to listen! Sometimes when we say prayers, we try to do all of the talking, but we also need to sit quietly and listen. God may use a voice to tell us something, or God can put an idea in our minds to think about or act on. God can even send a person to give us a message!**

God talks to us in many ways. We need to remember that God is always near. Our God is incredible! *(Praise God!)*

Remember that God sent Elijah back to God's people, the Israelites. It is important to be around other people who believe in God. God may use another follower to speak to us or help us with a problem. Who do you talk to when you have a problem or are afraid? *(Let the children answer.)* **God has given you these people to help you.**

We use the word fellowship to talk about spending time with other followers of God. During times of fellowship we can hear the incredible things God has done, and we can praise God.

Materials

☆ twelve white paper plates (one set per group of three or four children)

☆ marker

Preparation

★ Identify one of the plates as "Earth," either by coloring it like a globe or by labeling it.

★ Write one word from the Bible verse on each of ten remaining plates. Write the Bible verse reference on the last plate. These eleven plates represent the moon as it orbits Earth.

Bible Booster

But for me it is good to be near God. (Psalm 73:28a, NRSV)

Bible Booster Challenge

STORYTELLER: **Today's Bible Booster is Psalm 73:28a: "But for me it is good to be near God." It's easy to forget that God is near. We might think that we are all alone, that our problems are huge. We might get scared. But God is near, and God cares for us and loves us. It is important to remember, "But for me it is good to be near God."**

We talked in the first session about Earth. Did you know that Earth has a "pal" in the sky, something that is always there? It revolves, or moves, around the Earth and never leaves it. It never takes a vacation or a day off. Do you know what I'm talking about? (Let the children guess.) **That's right—the moon! God placed the moon in space to revolve around Earth. The moon is always there, even if you can't see it.**

You have a pal like the moon, too. It's God! God is always with you. God never goes on vacation or takes a day off.

But God is more than "there." God knows what we are dealing with in our lives. God knows when we are afraid and need help. We have learned from our adventure with Elijah that God will help us. We need to call on God and listen for God's response.

(Give each group of three or four children one set of twelve plates. The group must work together to arrange the words of the Bible Booster—the moons—in order, clockwise, around the plate labeled "Earth." When the challenge is complete, give each child a Scripture Treasure. Review the information on the back of the card, and point out how the picture on the front is a reminder that God is always near.)

Photo: Meaghan Porter

Galactic Blast: A Cosmic Adventure Praising God!

Sign the Scripture

Let's learn the Bible Booster using sign language.

(Teach the sign language and use it as you practice the Bible verse with the children. If time is running short, plan to teach the sign language during reflection time. Reproduce the page and give it to each reflection time pilot. Video of a leader saying the verse using sign language can be found on the Adventure Video DVD/CD-ROM.*)*

GOOD
Touch your fingers of your right hand to your lips, then put your right hand in your left hand, palms up.

ME
Point to yourself with your right index finger.

NEAR
With both hands curved, palms facing the body, and fingers pointing toward each other, bring the right hand toward the inside of the left hand.

GOD
With right hand open, palm facing left, make a shepherd's crook.

Extra! Extra! (Share these tidbits with your class.)

Elijah met God at Mt. Horeb (pronounced Ho-reb). Scholars believe this was another name for Mt. Sinai, the place where Moses received the Ten Commandments.

On his way to Mt. Horeb, Elijah traveled forty days and nights without food or water.

⭐ Closing

STORYTELLER: **Here's today's mission for you to do at home. We learned that it is good to be near God, and one way we can be near God is through prayer. I want you to have prayer time with God. Talk to God and be near God. Tell God about one of your fears, and ask God to help you not be afraid anymore. Don't forget to listen, too!**

When is a good time for you to pray? *(Let the children answer.)* **Where can you go to pray?** *(Let the children answer.)* **Those sound like great ideas. It is good to be near God!**

And remember to look up in the sky tonight and find the moon. Remember how the moon is always near Earth, just like God is always near you!

Let's close with a prayer. After I pray a sentence, I would like you to respond with, "It is good to be near you, God."

LEADER: **Dear God, thank you for bringing us together to learn about how you remain close to us and care for us.**

ALL: **It is good to be near you, God.**

LEADER: **Thank you for leading each one of us to Vacation Bible School.**

ALL: **It is good to be near you, God.**

LEADER: **Help us listen for your voice.**

ALL: **It is good to be near you, God.**

LEADER: **We will remember that you are our friend.**

ALL: **It is good to be near you, God.**

LEADER: **Continue to guide us during our time at VBS as we learn more about you.**

ALL: **It is good to be near you, God.**

LEADER: **We pray all of this to you, our incredible God. Amen.**

Mission: Elijah at Mt. Horeb

ELIJAH: **So what do you think about what just happened? Weren't you amazed?** *(Pause.)*

You act like you don't know what has happened. Didn't you see that? Didn't you hear that? Didn't you feel that? You didn't? Huh. You must think I'm crazy. But I know I'm not.

I am Elijah, a prophet of God. That means I am a person who hears special messages from God and tells other people what God wants them to know. Sometimes the news is good, and other times the news is tough. Either way, I guess I'm used to having unusual things happen to me. Are you sure you didn't feel or see or hear anything?

Well, I have had a rough time lately. I have been out here in the wilderness for about forty days. You see, Queen Jezebel is trying to kill me!

It's a long story. King Ahab and Queen Jezebel introduced an idol, a fake god, named Baal to God's people, the Israelites. Over time the Israelite people began to worship and put their trust in Baal.

As you can imagine, God did not like this at all. With God's help, I fought the Baal prophets and worked to bring the Israelites back to believing in God. This made Queen Jezebel very angry, and she sent a message that she was going to kill me.

All I could do was run. I wasn't sure I could trust anyone. I felt very alone and very frightened. I had no one to protect me. I've been out here for forty days.

I came upon this cave and went inside and fell asleep. God woke me up and asked me what I was doing here. I told God that I was a good servant and had done all that was asked of me. But I believed myself to be the last one who believed in God. I told God that people were after me and trying to kill me.

God asked me to step out of the cave, for God was about to pass by. I did as God asked. Now, this is the part I can't believe you missed!

I had been standing there for a moment when a fierce wind began to blow. I was sure God was in the wind, and I expected to hear God. But the wind got quiet. God was not in the wind.

After the wind stopped, it was quiet and still. Then I started noticing things around me shaking. Suddenly the ground began to shake, and I realized I was in the middle of a great earthquake. I was sure God was in the earthquake, but it stopped. God was not in the earthquake.

Then I saw a roaring fire in front of me. I was sure God would be in the fire, but no, God was not in the fire, either.

Once more, everything was still. Then I heard a quiet whisper. It was God!

God asked me again why I was here. I told God people were trying to kill me. God told me to go back to work. I am getting ready to go to a place near Damascus. God told me I would find seven thousand people there who still believe.

God could have chosen to forget about me. Instead, God talked to me in a simple, quiet voice. The wind, the earthquake, and the fire reminded me of God's power. But hearing the still small voice reminded me God cares about me and has work for me to do! Our God is incredible! *(Praise God!)*

Our God is big and powerful, but our God is also loving and personal. Now if you'll excuse me, I must go and do my work!

(Elijah leaves.)

Session 3

Mission
The Woman at the Well
(John 4:1-42)

Bible Booster
O Lord, you have searched me and known me.
(Psalm 139:1, NRSV)

Praise Phrase
Our God is amazing! Praise God!

Color of the Day
Blue

Mission: The Woman at the Well (John 4:1-42)

Materials

For every session
- ☆ *Activity Center Signs,* "Good News Galaxy" and "Praise Phrase"
- ☆ *Bible Storyteller & Sound Effects CD*
- ☆ CD player
- ☆ Bible
- ☆ *Bible Storyteller*
- ☆ Bible story costumes
- ☆ *Solar Key Chain* (one per child)

For this session
- ☆ *Decorating Transparencies,* "Biblical Town" and "Signpost" ("Sychar")
- ☆ plants and rocks
- ☆ thirty-two brown paper grocery bags
- ☆ newspapers (for stuffing bags)
- ☆ clear packing tape
- ☆ four small plastic buckets
- ☆ rope
- ☆ water
- ☆ paper cups (one per child)
- ☆ white carnation or daisy in plain water
- ☆ white carnation or daisy in blue water
- ☆ Session Three Bible verse printed on posterboard or the poster from the *Decorating Poster Pak*
- ☆ Session Three *Scripture Treasures:* Stars 3-D card (one per child)
- ☆ ten stars cut from yellow posterboard
- ☆ marker
- ☆ one yard of navy or black fabric
- ☆ ten safety pins
- ☆ ten pieces of string, varying from three to four feet in length
- ☆ ten paper clips

Photo: Lima Jo Simon

Creating the Atmosphere

Bible Adventure Room

★ Post the "Good News Galaxy" sign outside the room. Post the "Praise Phrase" sign with today's Praise Phrase ("Our God is amazing! Praise God!") in a prominent place inside the room.

★ On one of the walls, trace, paint, and hang the "Biblical Town" scene from the *Decorating Transparencies*. If possible, cover the entire wall with the full landscape so the children feel like they are outside the Bible town of Sychar when they arrive. See page 8 of the *Decorating Guide* for detailed instructions for creating backdrops from transparencies.

★ Use the "Signpost" *Decorating Transparency* to create a signpost indicating the direction of town. Use the "Sychar" label for today's lesson.

★ Place plants and rocks around the room. Keep these available for Sessions Four and Fve.

★ In the center of the room construct a stone well from grocery bags stuffed with newspaper. (See instructions for making the well.)

Constructing a Stone Well

★ To create the "stones," stuff brown paper grocery bags with newspapers, then seal the openings with the packing tape. For added effect, wrinkle the paper bags before stuffing them.

★ Stack the stones about three feet high in a circle with a diameter of about two feet. Place a bucket of water inside the well. Tie a rope to the handle of the bucket and drape it over the side of the well.

Drama Characters and Costumes

★ Jesus: Dress in a simple robe tied closed with a sash. Sandals are the appropriate footwear.

★ Samaritan Woman: Wear a simple robe in a muted color, a belt, and a head covering. She is carrying a bucket.

★ Jesus' Disciples: Dress in tunics, robes, and belts, all in muted colors.

Bible Booster Challenge

★ Write one word of the Bible Booster on each of the nine stars. Write the Bible verse reference on the tenth star. Punch a hole in the top of each star.

★ Hang the material on the wall. Pin the ten strings across the top of the material, attaching the paper clips to the other end of the strings.

Test Church Tip

We made our well from a trash can covered in brown and gray contact paper.

⭐ Story Starter

STORYTELLER: **Welcome back to the Good News Galaxy! Today we're visiting the town of Sychar** (pronounced SIGH-kar). **Before I tell you about this town, who remembered the special mission? Did you have a conversation with God?** (Allow a few children to share.) **Why did I ask you to talk to God?** (It is good to be near God.)

Did you look in the night sky and see the moon? What does the moon remind you of? (Let the children answer.) **The moon never leaves Earth. It revolves around Earth, no matter where Earth travels. In the same way, God never leaves our side. God is always near. Our God is incredible!** (Praise God!)

Today we are going to learn more about our wonderful and incredible God. Are you ready? (Yes!)

You've arrived in Sychar, a town in the land of Samaria. The road running through this town is very well traveled. It's the shortest route between Judea and Galilee, so many Jews walk along this road. The Jews are another name for the Israelites, God's chosen people.

The Jewish people and the people of Samaria, called Samaritans, don't like each other very much because they disagree on where to worship God. The Jews believe you have to worship God in Jerusalem, but the Samaritans believe you have to worship God at Mt. Gerizim (pronounced GER-uh-zim). **If a Jew and a Samaritan meet, you'll see that they aren't very friendly.**

Sychar was once the land of a follower of God named Jacob. Jacob had twelve sons who became the leaders of the twelve tribes of Israel. This particular town Jacob gave to one of his sons, Joseph.

(Point to the well.) **The water well here is called Jacob's well. It's about 135 feet deep, so it takes a very long rope to drop the bucket deep into the well.**

Many people from Sychar get their water from this well. It's about noon right now, so most people have already been to the well, or else they're planning to come this evening. They don't usually come for their water in the middle of the day.

People bring their own jars to the well. They fill their jars with water and carry them back to their homes. (Show an empty plastic bucket.) **If this were your water jar and you filled it with water, how would you carry it home?** (Ask one child to demonstrate what he or she would do; most children will carry the bucket their hands or arms.) **In Bible times, the people balanced the jar or bucket on their head to carry it back to their homes. Some people still do this today! Would you like to try?** (Let children try to balance the extra buckets on their heads and pretend to carry the water.)

Imagine you had to travel to the town well each day, fill the jar with water, and carry it home on your head. How would you like that chore? (Let the children respond.)

**Back to why we're in Sychar...
I wanted to be here because I
understand Jesus is going to
be passing through today. Do
you know who Jesus is?** *(Let the
children answer.)* **Jesus is God's
Son! Jesus has been traveling
throughout this area teaching,
performing miracles, and bringing
people closer to God.**

*(If you are using the single storyteller
version on page 37, begin it here and
pick up the lesson at the Bible Wrap-
Up on page 32.)*

Today's Cosmic Adventure

(Play track #16 from the Bible
Storyteller & Sound Effects CD.
Jesus enters and sits by the well.)

STORYTELLER: **There he is! That's
Jesus. Maybe he'll teach today.**

*(The Samaritan woman enters and
goes to the well.)*

JESUS: **Would you give me a drink?**

SAMARITAN WOMAN: **Why are you, a
Jew, asking me for a drink?**

STORYTELLER: *(To the children)* **This
could be trouble! A Jew isn't
supposed to talk to a Samaritan. I
wonder what Jesus is doing?**

JESUS: **If you knew who I was, and
the gift of God that I could give
you, then** *you* **would be asking** *me*
for a drink of living water.

SAMARITAN WOMAN: *(Looking where
Jesus is sitting)* **You don't have a
bucket, and this well is very deep.
Where are you going to find this
living water? Are you greater than
Jacob, the great follower of God?**

JESUS: **Everyone who drinks the
water from this well will be thirsty
again. But if you drink the water I
have, you will never be thirsty.**

SAMARITAN WOMAN: *(Excited)* **I want
this water you have! I never want
to be thirsty again or have to keep
coming here to draw water.**

JESUS: **Go and tell your husband to
join us.**

STORYTELLER: *(To the children)* **This
conversation is getting deep!
Jesus wants her husband here
because in these times, a man
should not be having such a
serious conversation with a
woman without her husband
present.**

SAMARITAN WOMAN: **I don't have a
husband.**

JESUS: **You are right. In fact you
had five husbands, and the man
you are living with right now is not
your husband.**

STORYTELLER: *(To the children)* **She
might be a widow. It's a custom in
Bible times that a woman would
marry her husband's brother if
her husband dies. Maybe the man
she is living with now is another
brother. I don't know, but it doesn't
really matter. What's important
is this: How does Jesus know so
much about her, a woman he just
met?**

Test Church Tip

In this drama adaptation,
the Bible storyteller acts as
an intermediary between
the children and the action
happening in front of
them. The children were
particularly engaged in the
story because the storyteller
explained each interchange
in a gossip-like way. When
Jesus asked the woman
to see her husband, the
children said, "Oooh!"
even before the storyteller
explained why!

SAMARITAN WOMAN: *(Surprised)* **I see you are a prophet, for what you say about me is true. So if you are a prophet, tell me where we should worship God. The Jews say we should worship in Jerusalem, and the Samaritans say we should worship on Mt. Gerizim. Who is right?**

STORYTELLER: *(To the children)* **Remember what I told you a moment ago? This is the question that has caused problems between the Samaritan people and the Jews. She has asked Jesus to tell her the right answer. Let's see what he says.**

JESUS: **The time is coming when we will not worship God in just a temple in Jerusalem or on top of a mountain. The time is here when we must worship God in truth and spirit.**

SAMARITAN WOMAN: **I know that God's Son is coming, and when he comes he will tell us all that we need to know.**

JESUS: **I am he, the one who is speaking to you. I am God's Son!**

(The Samaritan woman stares at Jesus, surprised. Just as she is about to speak, two disciples enter and begin to talk to Jesus in hushed tones. The Samaritan woman walks over to the children.)

SAMARITAN WOMAN: *(To the children)* **Do you believe this man could be the Son of God? Is that possible? You heard him tell me things about myself that others don't know. How did he know them? What do you think?** *(Let the children answer.)*

This is amazing news! I must go and tell everyone in town about Jesus! *(To Jesus)* **Jesus, please stay in Sychar with us for a few days. I want everyone to meet you.**

(Jesus agrees. Jesus, the disciples, and the woman leave the room.

SAMARITAN WOMAN: *(As she exits)* **Come and see this man who has told me everything I have ever done!**

(Turn off the Bible Storyteller & Sound Effects CD.*)*

★ Bible Wrap-Up

STORYTELLER: **She is very excited, isn't she? What is she doing?** *(She's telling others about Jesus.)* **Yes, she wants others to experience Jesus just as she did. Our God is amazing!** *(Praise God!)*

What do you think excited the woman the most? What made her believe that Jesus is the Son of God? *(Let the children share their ideas.)*

Jesus surprised the woman many times. Let's make a list.
(The list might be as follows:
★ *Jesus surprised the woman by talking to her at all, because Jews and Samaritans didn't speak to each other.*
★ *Jesus surprised her by offering to give her a special kind of water so she would never be thirsty again.*
★ *Jesus surprised her when he told her about her past.*
★ *Jesus surprised her when he told her he was the Son of God.)*

Jesus is the Son of God, so Jesus has the same power and knowledge as God. Jesus and God both know us and everything about us, just like Jesus knew all about this woman.

Another time, Jesus tells his followers, "And even the hairs on your head are all counted" (Matthew 10:30). That tells me that God knows more about me than I know about myself!

Jesus knows so much about us because he cares about us and loves us. The woman was so excited to find out that he knew about her life. She just had to share the news of knowing Jesus with others! She praised Jesus throughout the town, and the Bible tells us that she brought many people to Jesus. When they met him, many more believed that he is the Savior of world. You can read the woman's story in the New Testament, starting in John 4:1.

Our response to knowing Jesus should be like the woman's response. We know the loving God who sent his Son to be our Savior. This is good news we should share with everyone. Our God is amazing! (Praise God!)

Life Application

STORYTELLER: **Is anyone thirsty?** (With the help of another adult in the room, raise the bucket of water from the well and fill the children's cups.) **Jesus told the woman at the well that he could offer her some living water that would keep her from being thirsty ever again. Do you think there is special water that you can drink so you will never need another drink again?** (No.) **So what do you think Jesus was talking about?** (Let the children share their ideas.)

Jesus didn't mean that this woman would never have to come to the well again. He wanted her to know that if she filled her life with Jesus, believed in him as God's Son, and knew he came to this world as our Savior, he would always be with her to help her.

(Show the children the two flowers.) **These flowers can give you an** idea of what it might mean to be filled with Jesus in your life. Flowers need water to survive. One flower is in plain water, and it looks like it has always looked. I added food coloring to the water the other flower By doing this, I was able to change the flower's color.

Being filled with Jesus made a difference in the Samaritan woman's life. After meeting Jesus and believing that he is God's Son, she shared her good news with the townspeople. She brought others to Jesus, and her life was filled with him. Something changed on the inside, and people could see it on the outside.

What could you do on the outside to show Jesus has changed you on the inside? (Discuss ideas with the children.)

Materials

☆ ten stars cut from yellow posterboard
☆ marker
☆ one yard of navy or black fabric
☆ ten safety pins
☆ ten paper clips
☆ ten pieces of string, varying from three to four feet in length

Preparation

★ Write one word of the Bible verse on each of the nine stars. Write the Bible verse reference on the tenth star. Punch a hole in the top of each star.
★ Hang the material on the wall. Pin the ten strings across the top of the material, attaching the paper clips to the other end of the strings.

Bible Booster

O LORD, you have searched me and known me. (Psalm 139:1, NRSV)

Bible Booster

STORYTELLER: **We learned in the first session how God created everything and gave everything its place. People who have studied the stars over the centuries have learned that the stars are in special formations. The stars aren't scattered around; instead, they appear in these same formations, called constellations, each and every night. Because the stars are always in the same patterns, people can use the stars to know what time of year it is and what direction they're facing.**

God knows where every star is because God put the stars in their constellations. When you look up at the sky and see all the stars, think about the fact that God placed each star in the sky to be in a certain place every night. If God can care about the placement of each one of the billions of stars, think about how much God cares about the lives of each one of the billions of people on Earth. God knows you just like God knows where every star is. Our God is amazing! *(Praise God!)*

Today's Bible Booster is Psalm 139:1: "O LORD, you have searched me and known me." This Bible verse reminds us that God and Jesus know us very well.

I have put one word from the Bible Booster on each of these ten stars. Let's hang the stars in the correct order so we can read the verse together.

(Give ten children a star; have the other children direct the star holders where to hang them. Ask those holding the stars to hang the stars on the clips in the correct order. Upon completion, read the verse together. Then give each child a Scripture Treasure. Review the information on the back of the card, and point out how the picture on the front is a reminder that God knows each of us just like God knows each star.)

(Share this tidbit with your class.)

The Samaritan woman made many of her fellow townspeople interested in Jesus, but they didn't believe that he was the Son of God until they met him themselves. A personal relationship with Jesus is life-changing!

Photo: Meaghan Porter

Sign the Scripture

Let's learn the Bible Booster using sign language.

(Teach the sign language and use it as you practice the Bible verse with the children. If time is running short, plan to teach the sign language during reflection time. Reproduce the page and give it to each reflection time pilot. Video of a leader saying the verse using sign language can be found on the Adventure Video DVD/CD-ROM.)

LORD
Make an L with your right hand and bring it from left shoulder to right hip.

SEARCH
Make a C-shape with your right hand so that the palm faces left. Circle the C-shaped right hand counterclockwise in front of your face.

ME
Point to yourself with your right index finger.

KNOW
Tap your forehead with the fingertips of your right hand.

Photos: Matt Huesmann

 # Closing

STORYTELLER: **Before we go, I have another mission for you. You can tell me how you did when you come back. I want you to tell someone today about how well God knows you. Remember, just like Jesus knew all about the woman he met at the well, God knows all about you and loves you. Tell this person that our God is amazing!** *(Praise God!)* **If the person you tell is someone who isn't coming to church, you might want to invite him or her to come with you to learn about how God is wonderful, incredible, and amazing!** *(Praise God!)*

That's exactly what the Samaritan woman did. She went into town to introduce as many people as she could to Jesus. That's our job, too!

Let's close with a prayer. After I pray a sentence, I would like you to respond with, "Lord, you have searched me and known me."

LEADER: **Dear God, thank you for bringing us together at VBS so we can learn how much you know us and care for us.**

ALL: **Lord, you have searched me and known me.**

LEADER: **Thank you for the life of each child here, and help us remember to come to you when we need help.**

ALL: **Lord, you have searched me and known me.**

LEADER: **Help us remember to tell others about you and share your love with others.**

ALL: **Lord, you have searched me and known me.**

LEADER: **Continue to guide us during our time at VBS as we learn more about you.**

ALL: **Lord, you have searched me and known me.**

LEADER: **We pray all of this in Jesus' name. Amen.**

Photo: Meaghan Porter

Galactic Blast: A Cosmic Adventure Praising God!

Mission: The Woman at the Well
(Single Storyteller Version)

SAMARITAN WOMAN: **I must tell you about the man I met here earlier today! He has told me everything I have ever done! Is it possible he could be the Son of God?**

It was about noon, and I was coming to the well to get some water. I don't usually run into people at the well at this time of day, but a man was there. I could tell he was a Jew. You know that I am a Samaritan, so you also know he really shouldn't talk to me!

But he did talk to me. He asked me for a drink. I was shocked! I asked him why, since he was a Jew, he would be asking me for a drink. He answered me with the most curious response. He told me that if I really knew who he was, *I* would be asking *him* for a drink of living water. He told me that after a drink of his living water, I would never be thirsty again!

I asked him where he found this living water. "Do you really think you are greater than Jacob, our great follower of God?" I asked.

At that point he asked to speak to my husband. I think he wanted my husband here because the conversation was getting a bit personal.

I had to tell him that I don't have a husband. Then he really shocked me.

"You're right," he said. "You have had five husbands, and the man taking care of you right now is not your husband."

All of that is very true, but I didn't know how this man knew so much about me. I thought he must be a prophet, so I decided to ask him an important question. One of the things that separates the Samaritans from the Jews is where they choose to worship. The Samaritans believe they should worship on Mt. Gerizim, and the Jews believe they should worship in Jerusalem. So I asked him who was right.

The man told me that the time is coming when everyone will not worship God just in a temple in Jerusalem or on top of a mountain. He said we must worship God in truth and spirit.

From that answer, I knew this man was someone special! I said that I believed God's Son was coming and that he would teach us and give us salvation for eternal life. Then an amazing thing happened: The man told me that *he* was God's Son!

I was shocked. Here I was, standing at a well, and God's only Son was asking me for a drink!

Do you believe this man could be the Son of God? Is that possible? He told me things about myself that others don't know. How did *he* know them?

I must go and tell everyone in the town about Jesus. I have asked him to stay for a few days and teach us all we need to know. What an amazing chance to get to know God's Son!

(The woman leaves.)

Mission
A Blind Beggar in Jericho
(Luke 18:35-43)

Bible Booster
The voice of the LORD is powerful; the voice of the LORD is full of majesty.
(Psalm 29:4, NRSV)

Praise Phrase
Our God is magnificent! Praise God!

Color of the Day
Yellow

Mission
A Blind Beggar in Jericho (Luke 18:35-43)

★ Materials

For every session
- ☆ *Activity Center Signs,* "Good News Galaxy" and "Praise Phrase"
- ☆ *Bible Storyteller & Sound Effects CD*

- ☆ CD player
- ☆ Bible
- ☆ *Bible Storyteller*
- ☆ Bible story costumes

- ☆ *Solar Key Chain* (one per child)

For this session
- ☆ *Decorating Transparencies,* "Biblical Town" and "Signpost" ("Jericho")
- ☆ plants and rocks
- ☆ blindfolds (one per child)
- ☆ Session Four Bible verse printed on posterboard or the poster from the *Decorating Poster Pak*

- ☆ Session Four *Scripture Treasures:* Comet 3-D card (one per child)
- ☆ seven cardboard circles, two feet in diameter
- ☆ aluminum foil
- ☆ permanent marker

Photo: Lima Jo Simon

Creating the Atmosphere

Bible Adventure Room

★ Post the "Good News Galaxy" sign outside the room. Post the "Praise Phrase" sign with today's Praise Phrase ("Our God is magnificent! Praise God!") in a prominent place inside the room.

★ Use the same backdrop as prepared for Session Three. Rearrange the plants and rocks to give the room a different look. Remove the well.

★ Change the sign on the signpost to indicate that the location is now Jericho.

Drama Characters and Costumes

★ Jesus: Dress in a simple robe tied closed with a sash. Sandals are the appropriate footwear.

★ Blind Beggar: Dress in a ragged, wrinkled, dirty tunic of a muted color, and carry a cane. The beggar has messy hair and a dirty face and generally looks unkempt.

★ Children: The children play the role of townspeople. Tunics, robes, and belts, all in muted colors, are appropriate attire.

Bible Booster Challenge

★ Cover one side of each circle with aluminum foil; let the cardboard show on the other side.

★ Use a permanent marker to write a few words from the Bible verse on each foil-covered side of the circles. (Be sure to give the ink a few moments to dry before you touch it; it will smear until it is completely dry.) Because some of the phrases share the same words, number the phrases as shown.
   ★ (1) The voice
   ★ (2) of the LORD
   ★ (3) is powerful;
   ★ (4) the voice
   ★ (5) of the LORD
   ★ (6) is full of majesty.
   ★ (7) Psalm 29:4

Generous children at one church actually gave the beggar money and trinkets! The beggar donated the money to the church's mission offering at the end of the day.

Story Starter

(The blind beggar meets the children in the hallway as they travel to the Bible storytelling room. The beggar should be disruptive and a real annoyance to the children as he or she asks for money. When the beggar follows the children into the room, the adult helpers traveling with the children push the beggar toward the back, hushing him or her.)

STORYTELLER: **Hello, cadets! I'm excited to welcome you back to Good News Galaxy. Before I tell you about today's adventure, I want to see who remembered to tell someone about how well God knows you.** *(Let the children share.)* **Did anyone invite a friend to come to church to learn more about God?** *(Let the children respond.)*

We've had an exciting time finding out that our God is wonderful! *(Praise God!)* **Our God is incredible!** *(Praise God!)* **Our God is amazing!** *(Praise God!)*

We learned how God created everything, and that God is still creating today. We also learned that even though God is huge and powerful, God is near us. God stayed near Elijah and helped him through a difficult time. God knows all about us, which we learned when we met Jesus, God's Son, who knew all about the woman he spoke with at the well.

Today's adventure takes place here, on the road to Jericho. I heard that Jesus will be traveling this road today, and I thought we might run into him again.

(If you are using the single storyteller version on page 47, begin it here and pick up the lesson at the Bible Wrap-Up on page 42.)

It seems like wherever Jesus goes, huge crowds follow, so it might get a little loud in here when he arrives. If it gets too loud, I will pass messages to one of you, who can pass it to the next person, and so on down the line.

Photo: Matt Huesmann

Praise God!

Galactic Blast: A Cosmic Adventure Praising God!

Today's Cosmic Adventure

(Play track #18 on the Bible Storyteller & Sound Effects CD. Gradually increase the volume to make it sound like Jesus is getting closer. Jesus enters once the crowd noise is at its loudest.

Invite the children to stand as Jesus comes in. The children form a barrier between Jesus and the beggar, who is at the back of the room. Jesus speaks softly to the children but the crowd noise drowns him out.

The blind beggar's questions add to the noisiness. The storyteller passes the answers to the beggar's questions through the children— similar to the game of "Telephone"— until the answers reach the beggar.)

BLIND BEGGAR: **Why is it so loud in here? What's happening?** *(The beggar continues to ask the question until the response arrives.)*

STORYTELLER: *(Whispering to the first person)* **Tell the blind beggar it is Jesus who has just come in.** *(Be sure the message moves back to the beggar. If the group is large, the storyteller may need to give the message to several children so everyone hears it.)*

BLIND BEGGAR: *(Shouting, after the message has been received)* **Jesus, have mercy on me!**

STORYTELLER: **Tell that beggar to be quiet!**

(The children pass the message back to the beggar, who ignores it. Turn down the crowd noise so Jesus can be heard.)

JESUS: **Who is back there shouting for me?**

STORYTELLER: **Oh, it's just a blind beggar who followed the children.**

JESUS: **Help the beggar come to me.**

STORYTELLER: *(To the children)* **Pass the blind beggar to the front to Jesus.**

(Be sure that all the children help guide the beggar to the front of the room. The beggar kneels in front of Jesus.)

JESUS: **What do you want me to do for you?**

BLIND BEGGAR: **Lord, let me see again!**

JESUS: **Then see again. Your faith has saved you.**

BLIND BEGGAR: *(Rubs his or her eyes, squints, and looks around the room)* **I can see again! Jesus has healed me! I can see you! Our God is magnificent!**

CHILDREN: **Praise God!**

(Jesus exits. The blind beggar follows, still praising God.)

Bible Wrap-Up

STORYTELLER: **How did the blind beggar know Jesus?** *(Let the children answer.)* **The Bible story, which is found in the New Testament beginning in Luke 18:35, doesn't tell us how the beggar knew Jesus.** *(Show the children the Bible passage.)* **It's possible that the beggar overheard other people talking about Jesus and his magnificent works.**

The beggar knew that Jesus was more than just a teacher or a healer; the beggar recognized Jesus as the Son of God. The beggar knew that Jesus could heal his blindness. He had faith, and his faith is what healed him.

(Hand each child a blindfold. Adults traveling with the children can assist in putting the blindfolds on.)

Pretend for a moment that you can't see anything. I'm going to play the crowd noise again. Imagine yourself as the blind beggar. *(Play the crowd noise softly.)* **You've been sitting along this road asking for money and for help. You can tell more people are gathering around you because the crowd is getting louder and more excited.** *(Turn up the volume on the CD player.)* **Naturally, you're going to ask someone to tell you what's going on, aren't you? Then someone says Jesus is coming.**

The crowd is big and loud, but you want Jesus to notice you. You can't see him, but you want him to see you. Try shouting to Jesus over the noise. *(Have the children shout for Jesus to notice them. Then turn down the volume on the CD player.)*

Now you hear Jesus' voice. He says, "Bring the blind person to me."

This is your chance. Jesus has noticed you! You must be feeling very excited. You can't see anything, but you feel people moving you through the crowd. You know you are about to be in front of Jesus. How exciting!

You hear Jesus say, "What do you want me to do for you?" You still can't see anything, but you know that you are right in front of Jesus. What do you say to Jesus? *(Let the children answer.)*

You ask Jesus to let you see again. You know that Jesus has the power to give you back your sight. Right away, Jesus says, "Receive your sight." Immediately, you can see again! *(Have the children remove their blindfolds.)* **Our God is magnificent!** *(Praise God!)*

(Turn off the Bible Storyteller & Sound Effects CD.*)*

Life Application

STORYTELLER: **Take your blindfold and wrap it around your wrist, or tie it like a bandana around your neck. Keep it attached to you for the rest of the day. When you look at the blindfold, remember that Jesus cares about you just like he cared about the blind beggar.**

You might think that the blind beggar had very little, but he had his faith in God. His faith blessed him and made him very rich in ways that can't be measured in money. What are some of these ways? *(Let the children answer.)* **His faith literally changed his life!**

The crowd tried to quiet the beggar. They didn't think the beggar was important enough to bother Jesus. But to Jesus, everyone is important!

You might have times when you feel like you are not important. Maybe you've gotten in trouble, or your friends are mad at you, or you're not getting along with your parents. But Jesus loves you, and Jesus thinks you are very important. You can always call out to Jesus for help, and when you do, have faith like the blind beggar's and know that Jesus hears you and will help you.

When you're close to Jesus and have Jesus in your heart, he changes you. Knowing Jesus doesn't mean you won't have problems in your life, but it does mean that you'll face those problems in a different way. You'll know that you're not alone. With Jesus, you can handle any problem!

Teaching healing stories to children can be challenging because God does not always heal by taking away the symptoms. One Bible storyteller explained to the children that God heals in many different ways, including by giving us the intelligence to make tools to help people who can't see well (glasses and Braille) or walk well (wheelchairs and crutches). "I had one child in my class who has muscular dystrophy," she said. "He uses a power wheelchair specially built for him. We talked about how God creates and works through the scientists and inventors to help people with disabilities."

Photo: Matt Huesmann

(Share this tidbit with your class.)

The Gospel of Luke doesn't tell us the blind beggar's name. However, this same story appears in the Gospel of Mark. In Mark's version, the beggar's name is Bartimaeus.

Materials

☆ seven cardboard circles, two feet in diameter
☆ aluminum foil
☆ permanent marker

Preparation

★ Cover one side of each circle with aluminum foil; let the cardboard show on the other side.

★ Use a permanent marker to write a few words from the Bible verse on each foil-covered side of the circles. (Be sure to give the ink a few moments to dry before you touch it; it will smear until it is completely dry.) Because some of the phrases share the same words, number the phrases as shown.
  ★ (1) The voice
  ★ (2) of the LORD
  ★ (3) is powerful;
  ★ (4) the voice
  ★ (5) of the LORD
  ★ (6) is full of majesty.
  ★ (7) Psalm 29:4

Bible Booster

The voice of the LORD is powerful; the voice of the LORD is full of majesty. (Psalm 29:4, NRSV)

★ Bible Booster Challenge

STORYTELLER: **Today we're going to talk about the special relationship between comets and the sun.**

Comets are a collection of ice, dirt, and rock. Think of them as "dirty snowballs" that orbit around the sun. The comets grow colder and their ice gets harder the farther they travel from the sun. But as comets get closer to the sun, the ice begins to thaw and the dirt particles glow in the reflection of the sun's light. The solar wind around the sun pushes the particles backward, which creates what looks like a tail. A comet's glow can be quite beautiful!

The comet becomes an amazing, glowing object in the sky as it gets closer to the sun. In the same way, we glow more brightly as Christians when we stay close to Jesus. We glow in the light of Jesus' love, and we can reflect that light to others. How do you think we can do that? (Let the children answer.) **Jesus changes us, just as the sun's heat changes the icy comet head into a beautiful glow in the sky.**

Jesus' voice gave the blind beggar his sight, but it was the beggar's faith in Jesus that allowed him to be healed. If we have faith in Jesus, Jesus can do amazing things in our lives. This Bible Booster reminds us of God's power and magnificent love.

Our Bible Booster Challenge is to create Comet Praise! Let's make a comet with seven volunteers.

(Hand each volunteer one of the large cardboard circles. Tell the children to hold the circles with the "dirty" cardboard side facing out. Alert the volunteers that each circle is numbered to help them know when to reveal the foil side.)

Pretend that our comet is coming closer to the sun. Ice particles are melting and picking up the sun's reflection. For our Comet Praise, we want the particles to break off in the order of our Bible Booster. So as the rest of us slowly say the verse, I want each volunteer holding a particle turn the circle over to the foil side to reveal the words of the verse.

(Say the verse slowly so the phrases can be revealed. The last circle to be revealed is the Bible reference, Psalm 29:4. Repeat the exercise, trying to say the verse more quickly each time. At the end of the exercise, give each child a Scripture Treasure. Review the information on the back of the card, and point out how the picture on the front is a reminder that a relationship with God changes us.)

⭐ Sign the Scripture

Let's learn the Bible Booster using sign language.

(Teach the sign language and use it as you practice the Bible verse with the children. If time is running short, plan to teach the sign language during reflection time. Reproduce the page and give it to each reflection time pilot. Video of a leader saying the verse using sign language can be found on the Adventure Video DVD/CD-ROM.)

VOICE
With two fingers of the right hand held in a V, trace the throat to the chin.

LORD
Make an L with your right hand and bring it from left shoulder to right hip.

POWERFUL
Strongly and sharply, lower hands in fists.

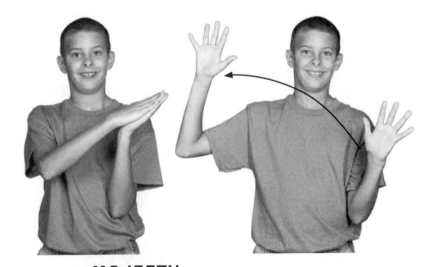

MAJESTY
Clap the hands together, then make an arc with the right hand, hand shaking.

★ Closing

STORYTELLER: **You have two missions today. Your first mission is to carry your blindfold with you for the rest of the day. Let the blindfold remind you how much God cares for you, just as Jesus cared for the blind beggar. Second, in response to knowing how much God loves you, I want you to show God's love to someone else. Jesus showed his love to the blind beggar by caring for him, but the way you show God's love can be much simpler. You can help someone out with a project or chore, tell someone you love them, or do something nice for someone in need. I can't wait to hear your stories!**

It's time to wrap up at the Good News Galaxy. Once again, God deserves all the praise we can give. God can make a blind man see, and God can do exciting things in your life, too! Our God is magnificent! *(Praise God!)*

Let's close with a prayer. After I pray a sentence, I would like you to respond with "O Lord, your voice is powerful and full of majesty." Let's pray.

LEADER: **Dear God, thank you for bringing us together at VBS for more time to praise you.**

ALL: **O Lord, your voice is powerful and full of majesty.**

LEADER: **Thank you for caring for the blind beggar and giving him his sight.**

ALL: **O Lord, your voice is powerful and full of majesty.**

LEADER: **Thank you for caring for each one of us.**

ALL: **O Lord, your voice is powerful and full of majesty.**

LEADER: **Help us share your love with others.**

ALL: **O Lord, your voice is powerful and full of majesty.**

LEADER: **Continue to guide us during our time at VBS as we learn more about you.**

ALL: **O Lord, your voice is powerful and full of majesty.**

LEADER: **We pray all of this in Jesus' name. Amen.**

God deserves all our praise!

Mission: A Blind Beggar in Jericho (Single Storyteller Version)

BLIND BEGGAR: **It is very good to "see" all of you today! Yes, I can see you all, and you all look tremendous!**

You know, just a bit ago I wouldn't have been able to see you—but now I can. You see *(chuckles)*, I have been a blind beggar all my life. For years I sat along the side of the road and begged for money because I could not see, I could not work, and I could not take care of myself. But as I sat along the road I heard stories about Jesus, God's Son. I heard how he was teaching people, healing people, and creating miracles.

I can remember wishing that Jesus would pass by me. I knew—I had faith—that if Jesus would just come near me, he could make me see. But how could that ever happen?

One day, I heard all sorts of noise. The people in the town seemed to be getting excited about something. I could feel a crowd gathering around where I sat on the road. I started to listen carefully to what they were saying, and I heard the name Jesus being mentioned over and over again.

I finally got someone's attention and asked him what was going on. He told me that Jesus was passing by. I immediately got excited. This was my chance to see! If I could just get his attention, I knew Jesus could heal my blindness.

I could tell the crowd was growing larger and louder. I was so afraid Jesus would pass by and never see me, this blind beggar on the side of the road.

I started to call out, "Jesus, have mercy on me!" I could hear people standing in front of me, between Jesus and me, ordering me to be quiet. But I couldn't let them stop me. This might be my only chance.

I believed that if Jesus heard me, he would heal me. I just needed to keep trying to get him to notice me. So I yelled even louder, "Jesus, have mercy on me!"

Suddenly the crowd got quiet. I could hear people stepping away from me. Then I heard Jesus' voice say to bring me to him. I started to shake. I was so excited. I was going to be in front of Jesus! Jesus heard me and was going to take care of me!

I could feel some people pick me up and help me to a different place. Then I heard Jesus' voice very close me. He asked me, "What do you want me to do for you?" All I said to Jesus was, "Lord, let me see again."

Jesus didn't touch me. All I heard him say was, "Receive your sight; your faith has saved you." And as soon as he said that I could see. It was a miracle!

I immediately followed him and glorified God. Everyone who saw the miracle joined me in praising God. Our God is magnificent! *(Praise God!)*

(The blind beggar leaves.)

Session 5

Mission:
Two Disciples in Emmaus (Luke 24:13-32)

Mission
Two Disciples in Emmaus
(Luke 24:13-32)

Bible Booster
The LORD lives! Praise be to my Rock! Exalted be God my Savior!
(Psalm 18:46, NIV)

Praise Phrase
Our God is awesome! Praise God!

Color of the Day
Purple

⭐Materials

For every session
- ☆ *Activity Center Signs,* "Good News Galaxy" and "Praise Phrase"
- ☆ *Bible Storyteller & Sound Effects CD*
- ☆ CD player
- ☆ Bible
- ☆ *Bible Storyteller*
- ☆ Bible story costumes
- ☆ *Solar Key Chain* (one per child)

For this session
- ☆ *Decorating Transparencies,* "Biblical House" and "Signpost" ("Emmaus")
- ☆ plants and rocks
- ☆ table and chairs
- ☆ bread (enough for everyone to have a small piece)
- ☆ Session Five Bible verse printed on posterboard or the poster from the *Decorating Poster Pak*
- ☆ Session Five *Scripture Treasure:* Supernova 3-D card (one per child)
- ☆ large, dark-colored sheet or shower curtain
- ☆ silver or yellow paint
- ☆ permanent marker
- ☆ small stars cut from yellow or silver paper
- ☆ washable markers

Photo: Staff

★ Creating the Atmosphere

Bible Adventure Room

★ Post the "Good News Galaxy" sign outside the room. Post the "Praise Phrase" sign with today's Praise Phrase ("Our God is awesome! Praise God!") in a prominent place inside the room.

★ On one of the walls, trace, paint, and hang the scene from the "Biblical House" *Decorating Transparency*. If possible, cover the entire wall with the full landscape so the children feel like they are on a road leading to the disciples' house in Emmaus. See page 8 of the *Decorating Guide* for detailed instructions for creating backdrops.

★ Place the table and chairs in front of the house. Add plants and rocks around the room.

★ Change the sign on the signpost to indicate that the location is now Emmaus.

Drama Characters and Costumes

★ Jesus: Dress in a simple robe tied closed with a sash. Sandals are the appropriate footwear.

★ Cleopas and the Other Disciple: Dress in tunics of a muted color, belts, and sandals.

★ Children: The children portray other followers of Jesus. Dress them in tunics, robes, and belts, all in muted colors.

Bible Booster Challenge

★ Paint a large silver or yellow star in the center of the sheet or shower curtain. (Keep in mind the size of your VBS so the size of the star corresponds to the number of children involved in the activity.) Write the Bible Booster on the large star with permanent marker. Hang the sheet or shower curtain on a wall.

★ Before each group visits the Good News Galaxy, cover the Bible verse with small stars, allotting one per child. (Experiment with the best tape to use so the smaller stars can be removed without tearing or damaging the large star.) Add extra stars until the large star is completely covered.

★ Set out washable markers for the children to use to write their names on the smaller stars.

⭐ Story Starter

STORYTELLER: **Hello, cadets! In our last session you took a blindfold with you to remind you of the Bible story. Did any of you have someone ask you about your blindfold?** *(Let the children share their experiences. As they talk, the actor playing Jesus joins the group.)*

Before today's cosmic adventure, let's review all the Bible stories we've experienced so far.

What happened in our first session? *(God created everything.)* **Our God is wonderful!** *(Praise God!)*

What happened in our second session? *(God came to Elijah in a still small voice to help Elijah.)* **Even though God created everything, God is still very personal. God stays near us all the time. Our God is incredible!** *(Praise God!)*

What happened in our third session? *(We met Jesus, the Son of God, who knew all about the woman at the well. Jesus made himself known to her.)* **Our God is amazing!** *(Praise God!)*

What happened in our fourth session? *(Jesus gave the beggar back his sight because he had faith in Jesus.)* **Our God is magnificent!** *(Praise God!)*

Today is our last cosmic adventure in the Good News Galaxy. We're standing on a road between Jerusalem and a town about seven miles away called Emmaus.

I heard some news out of Jerusalem that Jesus was killed about three days ago. I can't believe it! I know some of his followers live in this house. They're on their way here from Jerusalem, so I thought they might be able to tell us what happened.

I hope the news isn't bad. Have you ever gotten news that has made you really sad? *(Let the children talk about the sad news they have received.)*

(If you are using the single storyteller version on the inside back cover, begin it here and pick up the lesson at the Bible Wrap-Up on page 52.)

News out of Jerusalem...

Today's Cosmic Adventure

(As the children are talking, the two disciples enter the room.)

JESUS: *(To the disciples)* **Can the two of you tell us what's been happening in Jerusalem?**

CLEOPAS: **Are you the only person who doesn't know?**

JESUS: **What are you talking about?**

OTHER DISCIPLE: **The news about Jesus! Jesus was a mighty prophet of God—**

CLEOPAS: **—and the chief priests and leaders said that Jesus had broken the law and should be arrested.**

OTHER DISCIPLE: **So they handed him over to the Roman government, who arrested him and crucified him on a cross.**

CLEOPAS: **After he died on the cross, some men took his body and laid it in a tomb. With the sabbath coming, they had to leave his body there. They rolled a big stone in front of the opening so no one would disturb the tomb.**

OTHER DISCIPLE: **This happened about three days ago. But earlier today some women in our group went to the tomb. They did not find Jesus' body. They said they saw an angel who told them Jesus was alive!**

CLEOPAS: **Others from our group went to the tomb and found it was just as the women said. No one can believe what has happened, and no one has seen Jesus.**

JESUS: **But if you believe everything the prophets told you about God's Son, doesn't what happened make sense? Jesus gave his life for all people so everyone can continue a relationship with God and live with God forever.**

(The disciples look at each other. Jesus starts to leave.)

OTHER DISCIPLE: *(To Jesus)* **Don't leave. This is our house. It's getting late, so would you like to stay with us and have something to eat?**

JESUS: **Thank you. I would be happy to stay.**

(One disciple goes into the house and brings out enough bread for everyone in the room. At the table, Jesus raises the bread as if to offer a blessing. The two disciples recognize Jesus, but do not speak. Jesus gives some of the bread to the leaders, who hand it out to the children. As the children are being served, Jesus quietly exits the room. The last to be served are the two disciples, who turn to look for Jesus and then look at each other in quiet amazement.)

CLEOPAS: *(To the children)* **Did you realize who that was? That was Jesus! He is alive! I should have recognized him much earlier. It was amazing the way he understood the Scriptures.**

OTHER DISCIPLE: **He was right here with us! We must be off to Jerusalem to tell everyone what has happened. Jesus is truly alive! Our God is awesome!** *(Praise God!)*

(The disciples exit.)

Bible Wrap-Up

STORYTELLER: **I thought we would be able to hear what happened from Jesus' followers, but instead we heard from Jesus himself!**

We first met Jesus when he was talking to the woman at the well in Sychar. Jesus told her he was God's Son. Then we saw Jesus give sight to a blind beggar on the road to Jericho. Even though the woman and the blind beggar believed in Jesus, there were people who did not believe that Jesus was God's Son, and these people had him arrested by the Roman guards. He was hung on a cross and left to die.

But the story doesn't end with Jesus' death. Our awesome God raised Jesus from the dead. After three days in a tomb, Jesus was alive again! When Jesus' followers went to check on his body, he was gone.

To show his followers that he was still alive, Jesus revealed himself to them in a variety of ways. The story you just experienced was one of those times when Jesus revealed himself to two followers to show that he was alive. You can read this story in the New Testament of the Bible, starting in Luke 24:13. *(Show the children the Bible passage.)*

After the two disciples realized they had just spent time with Jesus, what did they do? *(They left to tell others.)* **They immediately went back to Jerusalem to tell the other followers. They didn't stop to rest, even though they had just arrived home from their trip. This was really big news, and they needed to share it right away!**

(Share this tidbit with your class.)

The blind beggar in Jericho recognized Jesus even though he couldn't see Jesus. The two disciples in Emmaus didn't recognize Jesus, even though their eyes were working just fine! By explaining the meaning of the Scriptures, Jesus removes their blindness so they can see who he really is.

Life Application

STORYTELLER: **Listen to the good news that we are to believe and share with others.**

Jesus is the Son of God. Jesus came to earth as a perfect person and spent his time here teaching about how to live and how to love other people. He lived his life as an example for all of us to follow.

We all sin, which means we do things that do not please God. We need forgiveness from our sins so our sins do not separate us from God. Jesus gave his life to forgive us so we can continue a relationship with God and live with God forever in heaven. We call Jesus our Savior because he saves us from our sins.

It is important to remember that God did not end Jesus' story with his death. God was still at work. God resurrected Jesus, which means he brought Jesus back to life. Now Jesus lives forever with

God. Our God is awesome! *(Praise God.)*

If we believe in our hearts that Jesus is the Son of God, that he died for us to forgive us of our sins, and that he now lives forever with God, we will also live with God forever. This is the message of Good News Galaxy, and it's a message we should remember for the rest of our lives.

The excitement of this news makes us want to share it. We want everyone to have a relationship with Jesus, to hear this wonderful story, and to know our awesome God is close to them, knows them, cares about them, and loves them very much!

If you have a child ready to make a commitment to Jesus Christ, and you don't feel equipped to talk with him or her, create an opportunity for the child to speak with your minister or children's director.

This lifelong journey with Jesus can't be completely understood in a five-day VBS program. Introducing the journey to children and inviting them to be a part of it is just the beginning. Be prepared to help them through this journey long after VBS is over.

Photo: Matt Huesmann

Materials

☆ large, dark-colored sheet or shower curtain
☆ silver or yellow paint
☆ permanent marker
☆ small stars cut from yellow or silver paper
☆ washable markers

Preparation

★ Paint a large silver or yellow star in the center of the sheet or shower curtain. (Keep in mind the size of your VBS so the size of the star corresponds to the number of children involved in the activity.) Write the Bible verse on the large star with permanent marker. Hang the sheet or shower curtain on the wall.

★ Before each group visits the Good News Galaxy, cover the Bible verse with small stars, allotting one star per child. (Experiment with the best tape to use so the smaller stars can be removed without tearing or damaging the large star.) Add extra stars until the large star is completely covered.

★ Set out washable markers for the children to use to write their names on the smaller stars.

Bible Booster

The LORD lives! Praise be to my Rock! Exalted be God my Savior! (Psalm 18:46, NIV)

Bible Booster Challenge

STORYTELLER: **Today let's take a look at a supernova.**

A nova is a star that gets very bright and then slowly fades. A supernova is a star that gets extremely bright and seems to explode. When a supernova explodes, many of its colorful particles break away. Scientists believe that these particles make up new stars.

In a way, God did the same thing with Jesus. God gave us Jesus, God's only Son, to live among us and teach us, but Jesus did so much more. Jesus' life was a bright, shining example of how we should live a life that pleases God. Jesus was willing to die for us so we can continue a relationship with God.

Jesus is our supernova—except Jesus' light shines forever, and each of you is a part of that light. When you have Jesus in your heart, you live the life that Jesus wants you to live, and you share Jesus' love with others. You're like a bright particle that turns into a star for God.

The Bible tells us to be children of God and "shine like stars in the world" (Philippians 2:15). **Your mission as you leave VBS is to shine like a star for Jesus, sharing God's love with others and praising God.**

Our last Bible Booster is Psalm 18:46: "The LORD lives! Praise be to my Rock! Exalted be God my Savior!"

In this verse, what does the word "rock" mean? (God is the rock because God is strong and steady, and you can always count on God.)

What does the word "exalted" mean? (Exalted means to lift up, to give honor, to praise, and to elevate above all things. To exalt God means to put God above all things in your life and give God all of your praise.)

In today's challenge, we're going to create a supernova that's sending off energy to make new stars. Cadets, please take a smaller star off of the large star, write your name it, and tape it onto the backdrop next to the large star. As you do this, the Bible Booster will be revealed.

(Leave the named stars on the backdrop. Before each Bible story time, add new blank stars so the next group can complete the challenge. By the end of the day, the verse will be revealed, and all of the stars with the children's names will surround the large star. Move the banner into the assembly area so the children can see the finished product.

At the end of the exercise, give each child a Scripture Treasure. Review the information on the back of the card, and point out how the picture on the front is a reminder that Jesus gives us new life.)

⭐ Sign the Scripture

Let's learn the Bible Booster using sign language.

(Teach the sign language and use it as you practice the Bible verse with the children. If time is running short, plan to teach the sign language during reflection time. Reproduce the page and give it to each reflection time pilot. Video of a leader saying the verse using sign language can be found on the Adventure Video DVD/CD-ROM.)

LORD

Make an L with your right hand and bring it from left shoulder to right hip.

LIVE

Use index fingers of both hands to make L shapes, with index fingers pointing toward each other, at your waist. Draw your hands in this position up your chest.

PRAISE

Clap your hands several times.

GOD

With right hand open, palm facing left, make a shepherd's crook.

SAVIOR

Cross your open hands with your palms facing your body. Uncross your hands and close your fingers into fists, palms facing out; then draw hands down, palms facing each other, in two parallel lines.

 # Closing

STORYTELLER: **We've come to the end of our last cosmic adventure. We have praised our wonderful, incredible, amazing, magnificent, and awesome God!** *(Praise God!)*

Your mission is to praise God every day. Pray to God daily, tell God "I love you," thank God for the many things you have, ask God to help you, and praise God's name.

Be a supernova for God! Spread the love of Jesus to other people. Live your life showing others that Jesus lives in your heart. You can shine for Jesus every day!

We will close with prayer. After I complete a sentence I want you to respond with, "Praise be to you, my Savior."

Let's pray.

LEADER: **Dear God, we have come to the end of our week at VBS. Thank you for a wonderful time.**

ALL: **Praise be to you, my Savior.**

LEADER: **Help us continue to stay close you.**

ALL: **Praise be to you, my Savior.**

LEADER: **Help us share your love and your story with others as we shine like stars in the world.**

ALL: **Praise be to you, my Savior.**

LEADER: **Be with us as we leave this place, and let us carry you in our hearts always.**

ALL: **Praise be to you, my Savior.**

LEADER: **In Jesus' name we pray. Amen.**

Photo: Matt Huesmann